Gardening on Mars

BY THE SAME AUTHOR

Ghosts Struggle to Swim (2023)
Wide River (2020)

Jane Frank

Gardening on Mars

Shearsman Books

First published in the United Kingdom in 2025 by
Shearsman Books Ltd
PO Box 4239
Swindon
SN3 9FN

Shearsman Books Ltd Registered Office
30–31 St. James Place, Mangotsfield, Bristol BS16 9JB
(this address not for correspondence)

EU AUTHORISED REPRESENTATIVE:
Lightning Source France
1 Av. Johannes Gutenberg, 78310 Maurepas, France
Email: compliance@lightningsource.fr

www.shearsman.com

ISBN 978-1-84861-965-4

Copyright © Jane Frank 2025

The right of Jane Frank to be identified as the author
of this work, has been asserted by her in accordance with the
Copyrights, Designs and Patents Act of 1988.
All rights reserved.

Contents

I. A Clearing in the Forest

Mount Glorious on a Spring Afternoon That Felt Like Winter / 11
What We Won't Know / 12
A Clearing in the Forest / 13
Cathexis / 15
Questions I've Been Meaning to Ask Trees / 17
Dry, Fine Days / 18
Soft Fascination / 19
The Fall / 20
Tigers in Cambridge / 21
Iris / 22
Ghost Hill / 23
Complication / 24
Swarm of Blue Dots / 26
Western Beach Walk / 28
View from the Spa / 29
Dream / 30
Forever is a Pool with a False Floor / 31
Recollections of the Last Male Northern White Rhinoceros / 33
Fly or Swim / 34

II. Epics in the Sky

Hobart Reset / 37
Wandering Stars / 38
Smoke and Ocean / 39
Empty in the Middle / 40
Wild Birds, Eagle Junction / 41
Dream Birds / 42
Denouement Days / 43
The Bees / 44

Oxyrhynchus / 45
Walk to Hays Inlet / 46
Summer Break with Chiaroscuro / 47
We Fly / 51
Gone / 53
Sonderings / 54
Farsickness / 55
Gardening on Mars / 56
How to be Happier / 58

III. SPINNING COIN

Astral Fields / 63
Lonely Poem / 65
Lunch on Stormy Day with Visible and Invisible Lines / 67
From the West Wing / 69
Incantation / 70
Fugue / 72
From the Attic / 73
Spinning Coin, 1993 / 74
Through a Car Window / 75
The World is Cruel & Lovely / 76
Grounded / 77
Vernissage / 78
Night on Prison Island / 79
Unbreakable Line / 81
Survey / 83

IV. WHAT STARTS AND ENDS WITH SPACE

Watching Hang Gliders
with Leonardo da Vinci at Tamborine Mountain / 87
Sketch, Creek Lane Maryborough, 1978 / 89
Why This Messy Blue Paradise? / 90
Elysian / 92

What Starts and Ends with Space / 93
Afterlife / 95
Wrapped / 96
Palm Reading / 97
Truths About the Cosmos / 98
La Casa Azul / 99
Tate Cartoon: *I Don't Care!
I'd Rather Sink Than Call [X] For Help!* / 101
Girl with 1,000 Faces / 102
You do not see less by looking at
a field out of focus with a magnifying glass / 103
The End of the Experiment / 105

Notes and Acknowledgements / 108

for my boys

1

A Clearing in the Forest

Mount Glorious on a Spring afternoon that felt like winter

We weren't even walking for the usual reasons,
found ourselves in a crypt
of rainforest trees—
shinbone trunks rattling
in haphazard rows
down to a v-shaped
ravine soaking
frond-rust and stones.
Fallen logs with moss fur coats
rose by the sides of the path
like beasts
and we stroked them as if they were lost pets.
Light in that forest was a thing of memory:
even rain didn't reach us.
Sometimes walking can coax remembering—
one step at a time—
I thought I heard a lover's voice
but it must have been a bird
or the wind:
something seemed to guide us.
Far off, a tree crashed and shredded.
Wallabies screamed.
We were inside a snow globe
but it was raining leaves and small hard seeds.
No water fell across the rocks
where a waterfall had dried to red dust
but we waited for increments
of beauty to cheer us:
ticked off a gem green frog,
a tarantula's foyer,
tree ferns tucked in fig elbows,
a high crisscross nest—
the home of what we did not know.
Knowing so little can be a comfort:
there was horizontal rain falling
back at the car.

What We Won't Know

Abundance is everywhere, grassheads heavy with seed,
millions of tiny discs shining on the surface of the lake like starbursts.

In the shadows, at the edges, small brown ducks drift,
smudges of ink on watery fingers. The house of poetry

has walls in colours yet to be named: perhaps love is soft moss
underfoot, without slipping, the deepest green?

Dusk is the cool rich blue of pollinators after their day of creating.
Cuckoos drift across speckled cloud, their sky path recorded

on the surface. In the future, will their feathers be planted,
grow in the soil? Will the horses that drank here

have the faces of ferns? I'm eager for autumn's quiet kindness
after a year without seasons, of scorching heat.

One day, we will look outwards together in the same direction
so give words to me. I don't want anything else in your absence.

A Clearing in the Forest

(i) They arrive: the clouds a tilled field of pink & tan / a library of what they left behind shelved across the valley all the way to where the distant ocean is glaucous mist / Now at her insistence they thread themselves through the sun- needle's eye to where time stretches in a complicated but clever yoga pose / leaves supinating in silver here near their faces / brightening / calling heat to the mountain grasses (ii) Tree ferns twitch in the gully beyond the part-rotting bridge / *walk on the nails* she says / elkhorn artworks on caryatid trees that hold the canopy / the needing-healing world of them / there's a haptics of bark & mossy wallpaper / dwarf-furniture in a tiny raised clearing surrounded by branches of yellow carabeen where the boys sit / unthink / process syllables of light posted through a zircon green ceiling / the dam soft & tea-stained / a telepathic mouth of soft sounds with lily pad edges / they perch there a long time without speaking & watch a field of blue billygoat weed on a fresh air flat screen cut in the forest until dusk darkens the picture (iii) Wood-panelled rooms filled with bottles / firewood / pokers & tongs / framed prints of fan palms & orchids / a bed as lonely as a boat adrift / a hole cut into the night's endlessness as if she is looking down / seeing herself as a spa-bathed pink specimen in a square tank / the landscape outside noisy with alternate foraging & decay / the mountain air ravenous (iv) She's the only one awake except for five donkeys braying from the top of the hill / their heads golden / lustre spreading like a benediction through layers of gum saplings / at the workshop they'd spoken of time compressed / intensified space / the suggestiveness of circular form but all the lines are straight here / the insistent horizon / the uptight white trunks / so nothing seems to resolve back to a beginning she can recognise (v) At Gardners Falls she momentarily dozes / dreams of flowers appearing for the first time to blanket hillsides / host dynasties of bees / forest melting into foam / into laminar flow / liquid over rocks birthing turtles & catfish that swim sluggishly with her almost-grown sons (vi) There are buckets of tipping colour where showers chase the hills after heat like a tomb / cows strung together against dark embroidered fence edges / she expects a warm moonlight above the cabins that the trees can't smother / in a discreet place like this the moon is always alive / breathing / all of living a lantana tangle / it's a wonderful late sky / thick air with occasional hieroglyphic birds that remind her of those onion skin paper eves with fewer marks / that uncomplicated time when her boys were still small (vii) They leave: king parrot sentinel dispensing their guitar riffs like streamers to the forest's edge so now the three of them are interwoven with turpentine / brush box & tallowwood / a palomino dawn cantering to the east / & they can feel curves now / the undulating spine of the range unfurling beneath them to where the road back descends

Cathexis

       Something beautiful
       is hurtling at me
       I can't gather it in
       don't want to see it go
a whip bird calls:
sunlight pries insistently
through Picabeen palms
       it is moving past
       and around me
       like an arrow from a bow
vertiginous views
from hairpin bends
       I seem to wrap words
       around me as a form
       of protection
sky shuffling through
a colour wheel of violet
lemon, rose—
       shouldn't I be better
       than this by now?
rainforest: vast miracle.
earlier, the almost silence
of place and thought
       so much more behind
       than ahead—years I mean
a blue quandong grove:
wild ginger, flax lily, thick
ferns adorning forest floor
       am I whole? a collection
       of parts not adding?
wide buttress roots
provide places to flourish
       short breathed fear:

                subtracting of the last
                twenty years
it's not as dark as you'd
think, below the canopy
                Rilke says unhitch beauty
                from terror > aliveness
light gaps are rapidly
colonised: a fallen tree
means fast growth
                enjoy panic if you can
                catch it

Questions I've Been Meaning to Ask Trees

Three black birds gather in the right-angle fork
    of a tall tree beside the car
    by the creek at the bottom of the mountain drive
    where I have stopped
    to stretch my legs and capture the tawny
    patchwork canopy of foliage on my phone.

No angle or filter does the colour justice.

The slopes are draped with sleeves of silky oak
    the colour of brass.

I don't ever remember a season so vivid or musical.
    I had no idea there were so many sandwiched
    across this valley.

I've tried talking to trees before.

I want to ask them *if they ever feel stuck?*

if they notice our indifference or esteem as we pass?

feel our fleeting admiration when they flower?

what they feel in their earth-held hearts
    when our steps don't break the soil?

Dry, Fine Days

   Tonight, I won't care if I'm not forgiven
but wonder if the creekside cicadas have paused
to sleep or if the wallabies that watched us
from the bridge are lonely under an absent moon.
The tin roof creaks with a kind of weariness
but I noticed flame trees and red gums in flower
along the ridgelines before the day was stolen

   Tonight, I won't care if tomorrow is better,
won't knit mountain air into worry or ride
the rapids of misunderstanding. The tiles are cold
against my feet, the boards honey-cream.
There are only elements here—no ghosts—
but I can hear stars singing, very softy,
whole choirs of them crooning in harmony

   Tonight, I won't care if my good intentions
are smears on the walls of you. The scent of cut
grass still lingers, and wood smoke. Rosella bushes
make their confession through the cabin window.
The hanging chair you sat in swings, drums bamboo.
This night holds the fragrance of 1000 dry, fine days
that have come before, some that even survived fire.

Soft Fascination

These creatures have gentle
edges
  like the sunlight draining
the morning of fog
      and I feel
suddenly ashamed:
      the silence
of a whole mob resting together
in this half-shadowed
       glade
is deafening, trees braiding mid-
morning's hair, real
       brushing ideal
so a quiet love steals anything
sharp
  from the pincushion
of concerns I've been carrying
about
  and the grey kangaroos like
being photographed, I decide,
because they offer
       their prettiest
angles and the joeys make shy
eye contact
   with me though two
strong bucks closely watch
       from
the elbow of the creek that frames
this grassy place
     and for a half hour
we share the same silver leaves
for eyes

The Fall

after Arthur Boyd's 'Nebuchadnezzar on fire falling over a waterfall', 1966

In the upper course of the river
Where the mountains are steep
The hooked trees are thick with
Their feathery presence and after
Rain there is a lushness, a rush
And a plunge to the punchbowl
Below

My foot caught the sun – I flew
Too high and their yellow eyes,
The colour of the fire sky touched
Turquoise, magenta, watch me oxidise
At daybreak – limbs white hot and
Cascading ash

So I wish I'd listened. There, I said
It. I wish I could gulp time with
Flame and breathe back peace.
But they say nothing now – heads
Bowed, wings close by their sides
At the tops of the deathly pale
Trees

Nothing will change. There will be
Endless fires and storms and the
Sky will turn red and the waterfalls
Will run dry. There will be kinetic
Cold and this madness of my own
Making will end. People have
Climates too.
I will fall.

Tigers in Cambridge

It's not the spires that stay with you
but the houses
floating in gardens like boats, the sky

roughly under-painted blue, shells
and their rowers
over-decorated in garish sun, river falling—

swelling—like breath, dragonfly buzzing
an intermittent static
in your head. In the park, tigers lurk

in cherry trees, trunks striped black, leaves
daubed in single strokes
unattached to twigs or branches, deranged

amber eyes. Later, on the road north,
a perfunctory call
from a lonely phone box and beyond it,

a view of hell: rainbows arched across
an infinity
of wheat fields, the distant hills open cages.

Iris

after Deleuze and Guattari's A Thousand Plateaus

You are a rhizome (and perhaps,
when I reflect, you always were?)
that pushes up through the soil
on the stretched map before me—

You are between me and that wall,
that line of hills, that conversation—
intermezzo. There is not a single
way to find you so I won't think

Of our history as a narrative that
began with Grimm and magpies
and hot sweet tea. Instead, wait
until sad surfaces open, fissures fill—

For a transparent sheet that spreads,
sinks, leaves no immediate trace,
the deep colour growing beneath
and sprouting in its planar way.

I have learned to like the element
of surprise: the shimmer of the cease-
less white caps that roll and hide,
the blue of fields that are at first

Glance green, the familiar curl
of lashes sweeping my child's eye
with its own ocean of purple. Irises
don't have edges or endings.

Ghost Hill
for my father

Those safe hands
on the wheel as we reach the crest
now locked in mine
a last time
though I don't know it

I hold tight
air moves fast
over a sprawling quilt of greys and mint greens,
appliquéd felt gums,
blinking dams
a vast taffeta sky

At our pinnacle
the car leaves the road
just for a moment—flies—
bounce-lands on the sinew of tar
seamed to paddocks
and scattered farmhouse lights
those hands keep us inside the dusk edges
the scalloped fringe of power lines

a nurse says this is the grip
of one not ready to go

A strange contentment
as the unknowns
fade at last
and we hold the wheel together
for the final downhill ride

Complication

is understanding blood components
    on a graph—
the way they undulate,
    rise, fall—
and their relationship
    to the depth of your smile,
the pallor of your skin

the way families turn inside out
    the same way hands did
in that childhood game
    where the fingers
are the church
    and the steeple
and Christmas decorations
    have faded a bit
even when there's no
    daylight saving

and my heart's an engine
    needing constant work—
all those bits coming apart
    that need fitting back together
so there are parts piled
    around the room
along with Lego projects
    and skeletons of poems—

I'm reminded of the man
    next door's legs stuck
out from beneath his Holden
    for years on end
(or so it seemed), even on
    suffocating summer days

like this one when the train
    timetable is a maze
and fourteen across is a deep
    furrow in my day—

the clue is 'stargazers'.
    I'll wait until the light fades
and navigate the galaxies
    beyond the mango tree,
the nearest 4 light years
    or 5.87 trillion miles
so what I'm seeing there
    across this complicated gulf
of sky is decades old,
    still childishly bright.

Swarm of Blue Dots

She grew up beside a beach,
collected pippi shells
and bleached coral worn
into animal shapes,
waited for countless tides
to make sense of rockpools

Endurance divided into living
is carving a hollow
in the side of yourself
and filling it with whatever you can find
to see you through desire
and time

What is the name of that tree
with the fulsome leaves
she asks herself so many mornings?
Is it a lush forest of giant
greenery she thinks
she is waiting for?

Waiting is like gardening
at the edge of a wilderness:
beautiful ideas that might exist
are unreachable
but for occasional seeds
that she grows in pots on a shelf

There's an abstraction
about waiting, a chain of poems
without endings: she goes shopping
and she waits, walks the dog
and waits, watches a pink sun
evaporate beyond a plateau

The lilly-pillies are growing
in a savage heat that skipped
spring while light mirrors back
and forwards via the moon,
words faintly visible
in swarming blue dots of love
that fade and brighten

Western Beach Walk

The paper of the sunset that day
had a heavy tooth,

the charcoal sea loosened and freed,
a deep line where sea met sky.

      A whale breached far out
beyond ballerina mangroves
teetering at low tide.

      Our shadows outgrew us,
feet pushing wet sand against the wind,

the secret crossing intertidal territory
inhabited only by crabs.

      I often take a fine-tipped pen to that day,
sketch the buildings hardly visible
beneath the tree line,

her face shaded like the island,
with the acid frogs and sugar gliders
hidden in the canopy,

its swamp pools near the shore
where waterlilies hummed.

      As we walked back
through swamp oak and spinifex,
the sequence of nature more ours than before,

the dark mass of mainland
was a store of first memories
at our back.

View from the Spa
Kingfisher Bay, Easter 2019

After the drum of night rain there's only tree fern talk
        in the arm of morning. Sometimes I imagine the reverse-

rain clouds with lilac gums sucking hard facts until they
        dissolve. I see more clearly in the warm water of this ceramic

spa, an egg perched in its eyrie high on this island forest rise.
        I am undetailed, undescribed, reshapeable, ripe for newness

Vivid against the palette of sun, an iridescent beetle perches
        on my wrist. Ideas burst like fruit, like sky pineapples.

Distant cabin creatures creep—the largest, praying mantis teal
        arching its overcarriage—the green train of dawn whispers

along a jetty with fish darting beneath—slick silver imaginings,
        rememberings—a horizon of time to grow familiar with
                                          [what's new.

Dream

      A forest tumbles
into a spectral valley,
a river cuts its way
through a landscape's operatic grief.

      I walk for what seems a night
until there is a clearing in my dream,
stop to consult my palms up close,
read their venations.

      There are love letters rolled up in the hollows of trees
apologies from once-loves,
instructions too:
give the colours names.

      Mist rises lethargically, and I can see
the doubtful stretch of water now —
almost touch it.

      White spoonbills dredge weeds at the edges,
azure kingfishers and rainbow bee-eaters

      sing words sticky like honey,
sweet but scared.
Venus is vivid in a metallic sky
where portents flash like fire.

      I submerge myself in the water,
while the flames
rage above,
leap across the stones,

      wait for the forest to regrow.
This takes time
so I take a deep breath,
swim into the future.

Forever is a Pool with a False Floor

Take the shore road.
Try to ignore the light pivoting by degrees,
the slight tear in the lining of the sky
that makes reading it complicated,
clouds hard to fix.
You'll pass the stone cottages
with their expressive faces
and out in the river mouth there are redshank
and curlew but you won't want
the sympathy of birds, the freedom of their eye,
all their layers of reality not visible to you.
The shell beach is almost too white
littered, as it is, with heartbreak.
When you feel the crunch beneath your feet
you can almost remember
the curve of yourself again
but you are taking this walk from memory.
You were a different person then.
You wore a faux fur hat with exotic markings,
you drank lime green concoctions
in a martini glass
at the hotel perched on the hill,
had a boyfriend who shared
a birthday with Hitler.
Back then, you were homesick
for places you'd never been.
You read that in Victorian times
this was an important port—
now there are yachts and fishermen.
Of course, the island is still an exclamation
between the estuary's blue lungs
so sit on the bench a while,
meditate in deep aqua infallibility,
feel grateful to be here:
there are a sea of souls waiting for vacancies.

Colours bloom, commingle on granite outcrops,
pearlescent streams of skin
and family grow—all your thoughts wash together.
When you're ready, take the path between two stone walls.
Walk along the edges of crop fields,
not venturing into the tidal zone just here.
Cross a bridge over a small stream
and enter woodland:
you'll find highland cattle grazing
among pale musk flowers.
There are an anaphora of kissing gates.
Leave them as you find them.
You don't know yet about cyberchondria:
that is all ahead like the short, steep climb
to reach the site of an Iron Age hill fort.
From there, you can see the mountains
of the Lake District across the firth.
Follow the road back down to the water
which might be splashing against the rock wall
or dramatic at low tide with rockpools.
You'll pass houses
with multicoloured gardens
belonging to people who live undisturbed lives.
Walk through a tunnel of ferns.
Pass a moss-green tree that leans
into a startling blue view.
This is where the walk ends,
not back at the pub where you left your car.
Finish here where tides fiercely cross,
where memory wears down
in the ceaseless thrashing
of shingle and stone.

Recollections of the Last Male Northern White Rhinoceros

We have almost all migrated to a lush savanna of the imagination
where there is no need to treat nosebleeds, strokes, convulsions,
fevers, or sell jewellery and dagger handles. Now we are here,

some spare a thought for our square lips, broad chests, convivial
family lives that spanned millennia. My eyesight was always poor
and my memory of the serene grasslands has now almost faded:

the jackalberry and acacia, the asters and blazing stars, golden rods
and wild indigo, the sensation of purple needle grass against my slate
hide as I strolled the floodplains. What I can't forget or forgive

are the night vision scopes, the silenced weapons, the helicopters scarring
flawless skies. Before I crossed the last wide brown river, I appreciated
the Tinder account set up for me despite it being too late for love.

Who knows? IVF may return us from the far bank, or as hybrids
with rhinos from the south or as clones. You've frozen our velvet tissues
and sperm and oocytes, but isn't it best to remember us as the ones

who had to fall through time so others can graze the lands of coneflower
and psoralea, clover? Lurch in cool mud under a red forever sun.

Fly or Swim

A three-quarter moon is already hanging
over the old aerodrome and horse paddocks

but my head is crammed with the sea—
its sheen—mosaic edge against the island,

though I suppose these lilac-green grasses
are their own ocean and clouds of pink-

chested birds are gathering in the concave
between road and falldown fence.

Walking washes away the talk of loss
and change and loneliness so I step fast towards

dark clouds to the north. The horses have
already turned their bodies against them.

Lightning is a series of thin silver scars
but the rain will be short-lived. Rose-grey

birds fly across my path in the half-light
now, in a diagonal line towards the pines.

2

Epics in the Sky

Hobart Reset

Part of me hovers in icy harbour air. Beyond the skein of
streets, the peak glows orange.
Love just is

and we happen to be in the path of it. I walk for a long
time, trawlers cutting through silk,
drawn to the red crosses

of Dark Mofo. I photograph the moon, distracted by strings
of far shore lights, the Derwent a dark gallery.
The blackness

is deeper here, velvet-rich like in ancient times when people
read the heavens like a book. I think about
how Earth looks

from space, red with fire, imagine snowflakes decorating
the space between me and the mountains,
easier to remember

who I used to be if I'm willing to become a little lost / Up
early, I wander down Battery Point's narrow lanes
scooped by sea views,

sun shards bouncing off sandstone and brick around a circus
of haphazard cottages, houses tumbling backwards
to the white-capped mountain.

Gulls circle. I could run from here onto clouds. Ivory flat-
lands sprawl through the oval window,
flying home. Transparent

edges where, if you didn't watch your step, you might fall
through to a green hell—only distances matter,
sundrenched finish lines.

I look into screensaver eyes that know I will soon return,
an absurd happiness striking. Already, I am
shedding layers.

Wandering Stars

Nothing in the world is lovelier than sleep
he said, but the river lassoed
in sunlight under the mountain today
as we crossed on the ferry
was the nearest I've ever seen blue come to gold

I am collecting sunsets
because it is the season of saffron skies
and I bottle the purple clouds
like fruit to keep myself going
through the bland months,

can't help photographing
the closest peaks of the Great Dividing Range
sitting like ice cream scoops
above the endless picket fence by the railway line
at last light, big violet nasturtium

shapes floating high,
moon swinging underneath,
and as I walk I imagine the road spinning ahead,
think about the wandering stars
I heard about on a podcast when I couldn't sleep,

the ones expelled in a pinball game
between galaxies
People are a lot like stars—young or ancient—
many of us hanging at the edge of an open cluster,
shining in two directions

and on nights when sleep won't come
I think of the writers who built an eternity from it—
Hemingway's wild animals when vines
claw against my white bedroom blind
or Plath writing to the chink of milk bottles on her step

Smoke and Ocean

Figures from antiquity shiver
or swim through every poem
I read lately—
is it the only way to make sense
of that lion sun waiting
to pounce
or the gossamer coast
or the amber face
staring back from my beer
in the restaurant at the end
of the pier that juts into Port Philip Bay?

Where I imagine Melbourne is
under the streaked sky
there's a fire burning.
Now would be
a convenient point
to allude to Zeus or Leda
but trees on the far headland
are the wrong shape
and I can't imagine Daphne
foiling Apollo or Adonis
giving humanity a woody strength.

The gums perch on the edge
of this land without a hope
of tying my heart
to the centre of the world.
Their silhouette is too stark
against unbroken winter blue to be mystical.
There is only what I can see—
no visitations from beyond—
but I am relishing this chance
for the salt water that is everywhere
to fill the parts of me
where words haven't been reaching,
to rock a poem from the wash.

Empty in the Middle

The crossword clue is 'empty in the middle'
& I think of scattered thoughts & vacant heads,
excavations in walls of rock & omissions in
lists & spaced out summer days, of drained
tanks & houses left when leases ended &
tooth cavities & dents & dips & crazy ideas
that invade your brain & the way sadness digs,
digs, digs, of beautiful items worth nothing at
all & the indentations bodies make on pristine
hotel sheets, of cardboard cutouts & troughs on
the sea bed, of moon craters & potholes after
the floods & dinosaur bones exhumed from
the earth & plates licked clean, of apricot seeds
gouged out & adumbral garden corners &
vortexes in the air & memory lapses & a dearth
of warmth on winter nights & my ancestors'
graves in Cyprus shade, of echoes in time &
the rattling space you can feel around your
heart when there is still a deep kind of yearning

Wild Birds, Eagle Junction

after Georges Braque's 'Oiseaux', 1962

The wild birds all leave my mind at once when the train moves
    from the platform.

I lose myself in the archipelago of colour that is the city sun-
    wrapped in its river, think to myself

that if I travelled on this train every day, threading the suburbs
    on a line like beads,

it might stop the birds from nesting & the mornings might be light,
    whipped like buttercream.

I try not to notice the wild birds through the window as they soar
    over the arc of the bridge

in their low, elegant formations but everything is easier at a distance.
    The train sways as if plunging underwater

and my head is drained empty, only the gentle notifications
    about approaching stations

and which side to disembark. They will be waiting for me
    at my destination

—the wild birds— they will ruffle their feathers against my thoughts
    as I walk home against a flat sky.

Dream Birds

Birds rehearse songs in their sleep
like she practices kissing, their wings twitching
in time with the soft movement of her lips.

It is always birds in her dreams: zebra finches
& whip birds & brush turkeys that build nests
among her garden ferns by day but wear the faces of people.

The exhilaration of flight & the overwhelm of distance
means her brain is alight with positive & negative
sensations all at once [pink + blue = a dull aubergine purple:

a code for quietly existing] but all the time she knows
that her dreams are cave walls or skies where words
can be scratched in ochre chalk or dabbed with cloud,

where strange imaginations beat against the bones
of her being & that mostly, it is a migrating bird that visits—
one eye open, one closed—whispering instructions

for how to dream across thousands of miles
between hemispheres & she wonders if that bird
conjures her in turn, grounded beneath blankets & sheets

but with an avian face & feathers, also caught
between two lives, if the best of her, too,
belongs in the starry arena between places,

whether love burns its brightest
in the parallel lives
of the night?

Denouement Days

A flock of birds: tea leaves in the cup of sky. Confuse the prophets, keep warm, preserve your stamina for the difficult days. Embrace celestial strangeness with synchronised clouds of words. The music of flapping wings: a silent comfort. That winter of missing you, I wrote you 57 poems about pain and flowers, about a crazy lick of flame at the base of my brain that ignited dreams. You helped me release anxious spirals of sparrows into the void. But black holes were in our galaxy's heart. These denouement days, I am summoned by the moon: I donate to charities and cook my children nourishing meals. Now the rains have stopped, the sea is cold. At 3 a.m., unwritten pages float on it, mother-of-pearl squares in a surrealist painting. I call out across the greyness not expecting a reply. The coast is carved from salt and each beach is a short disconnected chapter where white gulls circle: tiny doses of life.

The Bees

Bees buzz with brio in abelia—I kneel near them
        on the lawn. I read somewhere that honeybees
can recognise human faces.

To them, humans are strange flowers. More shapes
        and patterns to remember on frantic days. Ka,
the imprint of the Egyptian soul after

death, took the form of a bee. I imagine the garden
        teeming with dead Egyptians that know my face.
In another time, they spooned honey

into the mouths of stone gods, embalmed their mummies
        in liquid gold, sealed sarcophagi with wax,
moved clay hives up and down the Nile on rafts.

The bees were carried here in sun tears. I sip my tea,
        feel guilty because the bees are working harder
than me. Yet experts say there are workers

and shirkers, even thrill-seekers. That their brains defy
        time. The sun is their compass and they see it even
through cloud. But today the sky is an imperforable

blue and allamanda flowers are prolific pure yellow.
        It is not easy to believe a friendly bee that has fallen
through time would sting. They may have flown

countless miles this morning, but the bees seem
        close to home.

Oxyrhynchus:

A desert where it never rains, far from any flood plain
so words and imaginings went there to die, not expecting
a rebirth after two millennia. From the buried monasteries

& mosques, the necropolis for sacred ibis and baboon
birds, papyrus spluttered from tightly packed beds once
unzipped, mathematical equations serried with sweet

recipes, grocery lists, invitations to dinner, spells like
the one that would make a man leave her & love you
for good, mummy middens with their cartonnage of Sappho

fragments & classic texts, caches of Christian doctrines,
the anaerobic letters of abandon that weren't ever meant
to be found. Had been thrown in the trash. Lost in landfill.

In the woodcut I saw online, there are tower ruins & a simple
sweep of dunes. Date palms. A monumental stone gate.
Like looking out a window:

                                       when I open mine, pages
flap & threaten to peel from their suburban dossier. A
subterranean headache today: layers of me compressed

beneath timetables and spreadsheets, unanswered texts,
vet bills, scribbled notes on the backs of used envelopes
about the way the butcherbirds in my garden fly, books

of Barcelona walks & best baby names, curling photographs
of relatives I never met, printouts about the potential adverse
effects of dope on the teenage brain. The catacombs of half-

written poems: a sheaf of first lines that I must once have
thought had potential.

Walk to Hays Inlet

Sublet to the sea:
watch a zoetrope of tide (with small
aluminium boats) wash up
against your confidence
if you have the time to stay and watch

      There's a bone deep acceptance
of a kind of beauty that only being
alone can bring—the salt-surrounded
tree you photograph is unreachable
but it indents itself

                      on the brackish
enamel of Bramble Bay where tiny lights
on the water are their own set of cells
Here where you can find
the horizon through the outflung
arms of a dead gum

                      at the water's edge,
everything makes more sense than when
you were lost in the rumble
between bridges and chanced upon a man
releasing ashes from an urn

                      So often
now, there's no one to witness
what you love most—
it's as if the sea has moved in

Summer Break with Chiaroscuro

   The hotel is white
    & the pines are green-black,
cream bougainvillea clinging
to a brick wall painted garnet,
    my wrist casting a shadow
    on the page:
I can see my hard outline
& feel your absent one

    I like the graffitied laneways
    carved through this place,
the botanical precision in brunet corners,
oboe & clarinet illuminating
wine bars that are caves of stone
    the exactness of the street angles
    somehow reassuring

Today there will be a wedding—
ivory against bottle green,
    against limestone walls
    steps, arches,
    against the stage set of diminishing years

Pearl & chalk energy:
beaches, gulls, stones—
    a blue so deep, far out, that the land
    is a fortress—
but in close, the water is the cyan of starfish

I kiss you with my mouth closed—
it is called dreaming—
    while a dry-eyed sun burns my face
    & oil tankers at the horizon
    are the markers of conscience,

        reminders of other distant shadows
I count sixteen of them:
eat fish the colour of snow

        At the wedding
        flowers with geometric stems
        will adorn the tables
as the guests sip spiced orange fizz,
a waft of rosemary in the air

        The bridal party will stand
        on a square of lawn
        that floats in space
        affecting an aloofness—
it could be any city,
any day—
        the theme of love & endurance
        repeated
        over & over

I am obsessed with the uneven edges
of words & thoughts,
don't want the teal sky to fall
        but a woman with a topaz necklace
        will tell me her body's story
        as we watch charcoal & silver figures writhe

Bathers beach, when empty,
is a lonely place—
        a yawn of sea,
        single figures
        crawling at its edge
a black submarine & a sandstone tower

Flowers & bottles
blow off tables
bowls of apricots scatter,

        guests wrap their shoulders & laugh into the wind,
        the afternoon's promises already gone
Sea mist has reached this stony hill
but night hides it

        Catching the train from the old port,
        I closed my eyes
        & listened to the names of stops
        that are the stories of other lives—
ocean passing to the west
in an endless crocheted sheet,
cars abandoned beside
roads & dunes,

boards & bodies embroidered
to the nation's bleach-frayed edge,
        the jewel box of sea
        a million sparkling points,
        last light jagged behind clouds
        of persimmon & pink

When we return, the sky is cut with stars,
giraffe-cranes reaching on tiptoes—
        this train will terminate here:
        it sounds forbidding

Sun swims around arrowed
clumps of conifers,
picking out the upward sweep
        of high branches
        between the street & the sea

        The air is dry here,
        the old hotel swaying
        around its casuarinaed corner

The only birds are angry crows that chant
as we sip coffee in the bistro by the park

>   A seed falls from the tree
>   with maple-shaped leaves
>   into my lap—
>   it is pale & whiskery

I will smuggle it back east
& plant it
in wet soil

We Fly

into night
on ghost wings

There are torn pages
that won't be read

their messages lost
in our rush to cross the country

outsmart the desert
alphabets

we are above a storm
unaffected

by what's below—
hold our ground in the sky

It's not easy to write
in this eggshell seat:

we are above the storm
but there are miles

of misunderstanding
beneath us

During takeoff I held
an imaginary hand

traced my boys' tanned faces
saw for a moment

my toes bare
my shoulders brown

the future
a warm destination

In the west the sun dyes
the mountains

white gold today—
the coldest colour

Gone
for Will Bishop

The trampoline was gone from his front garden.
      Birds and lizards gathered in fading sun on the dead grass.
Somewhere else, surely, rusty springs creaked
      and the boy was still singing, bounces being counted, random
questions flung at passers-by about dates
      of birthdays and what was on the menu for tea.
When the loss registered
      the suburb spun.

              In her head,
          over and over,
     up and down,
the painting of a black-faced lamb, asleep beside a spinning globe,
      a child's drawing pinned to a forest wall,
a single plume of cloud in a peacock sky,
      a dream voice murmuring that *birds must wear watches*
           from beneath a haystack of sleep.

Sonderings

There are epics written in the sky:
hieroglyphs on the chins of clouds,
libraries of air looming
over smokestacks and aerials,
even bats streaming east like ragged words.

    Has there been a skyspotter since the start of time?

The Dictionary of Obscure Sorrows
calls it 'sonder' but highway infinity
is a dizziness of overthinking:
tapping the souls of perfect strangers.

Cars are Pandora's boxes:
hold unknown languages,
inventories of thought,
sagas tunnelling through cities.
This evening's imaginings
are eternities hidden in codes of headlight.

    Will anyone else read the page of clouds with me tonight?

Farsickness

The moon is lemon shaped. It would take nine years to walk
there. They say the Milky Way smells of raspberries and rum.
Here, in the fading light, the sky is tender as soft skin. A stadium
of tessellated rocks stretches out into the smooth water towards
the islands of Moreton Bay. In my palm, casuarina seeds are
the currency of freedom. On Mercury, a day is as long as a year. Here,
the stars pool like dust in the sky, last sun at the scene's
centre a screen for cartoon credits. Venus spins backwards,
but I read that here, our days are growly gradually longer,
the planet's spin speed slowing each year. Does this mean we
can claw time back? On days when I can't make everything fit,
I remember the bonsai garden that struggled to grow in clay soil,
the draught board beside your whisky glass awaiting a move.
Seventy sextillion stars are visible through a telescope. I think
about stars we will never be able to see. In the fernery beneath
the verandah of the old house, there were thousands of white
stones on top of peat that shone in lunar light. Here, above
the horizon line, there are dozens of moving specks and I
wonder at the light-drenched prism of a bird's mind, and how
you can be nostalgic for places you have never been. Space is
utterly silent but this pen requires gravity for its quiet ink to flow.

Gardening on Mars
for Euan

On the night you turn eighteen
   you work at the restaurant
      I want to wait up for you
   but it is late:
sleep is a patient river
and I am drifting in a sky-slow boat,
   everywhere above me stars make words,
      unstopped bottles
   primed to explode at the edges
of what I understand
and all the time you are telling me things:
turtles blow bubbles but fish don't—

   We float on the brook now
   and you are waiting for late sun
to light up the magical forms of bass
in the places unshaded by paperbarks
   I am listening to your voice
      as we glide—always your voice—
   feeling thankful you are clever
and that you talk—not about AI
or echo chambers or fake news
   or lies that infect the soul—
      but about how fishing
   calms your fear:
dying is something only the living do
you tell me, and that *'quisqualis' is Latin
   for 'any such'* with pendant flowers
      that *change colour from white
   to red as they age—
they have the scent of toasted coconut!*

You picked them for me
   when you were seven
      so I believe you when you tell me that *dandelions*
  would grow better on Mars,
that *astrobiology students have practiced*
with potting mix from the Mojave Desert,
  matched Martian soil samples,
     that *only a few of Earth's hazardous chemicals*
  will need to be removed
Your voice is soft like a song playing:
the oceans there have dried up
  but there is water below the surface
     and vegetables will be grown in heat-
  pressurised greenhouses with compensation
for atmosphere, humidity, water, love
in that cold, dusty atmosphere

   Our boat is moving through the living room
     where a butcherbird
   has found itself trapped
and is desperately searching for an exit,
lights rocking in their cradles,
   so I am sure its razor sharp beak
     will take out your eye
   but *a bird from the east inside a house*
is a sign of inspiration
you are saying to me,
   your voice clear but faint now—
     wasps don't fly at night.

How to be Happier

Don't think about
                bullets in the brumbies' heads
                at the end of the snow season

the molten eyes
                of that buckskin standing with two
                grey roans somewhere

on the Kiandra Plains
                when it searched your face
                from the glossy pages

of the magazine article
                in the dogeared waiting room pile
                as you anticipated

a reminder about
                addressing high cholesterol:
                stamp out that image of rotting

carcasses by the waterway
                that raised concerns for hikers,
                the remains of those wild blameless

creatures gunned
                down by helicopter fire

                *

Keep sipping your coffee
                when you worry that your children
                will only remember your imperfections

and let Bourgeois'
>	*maman* spider crawl back
>	into your mind—

remember sun
>	walloping your back in the art
>	gallery forecourt, the spider's

nine-metre-high
>	ten-metre-wide frame wavering above you,
>	abdomen and thorax of gleaming

rubbed bronze
>	its unlikely balance on silly slender legs,
>	 a *maman* always restoring

what is torn —
>	equal parts creator, repairer,
>	protector, predator

>	*

Take a sanguine breath
>	and hold your ground
>	remembering that Hemingway said

no one you love
>	*is truly lost*—stop searching
>	for wonders,

augurs of the one
>	you miss in that glint of violet mountain
>	at first light or in the visiting

possum's sudden

                midnight stare and avoid overlooking
                autumn, a fleeting beauty

of bronze and red

                —a majestic gold-edged book
                or a tree before its branches

fall silent.

3

Spinning Coin

Astral Fields

Her view from here has changed—
  that infectious grin her son
  had is gone in glare

The new neighbours felled all the trees
  so she can see the flaking underbelly
  of the house next door,

a peroxide blonde woman cutting lunches
  through a dirty window,

a bandy-legged crow
  winking slyly from the roof

The birds are louder on despicable days,
  the traffic more sinister

but later she will celebrate this day—
  the first time the mercury
  has dropped

below twenty degrees this calendar year—
  by digging the carcasses

of dead mint and basil from the burnt
  garden, pulling the green

stems and roots of weeds—umbrella
  sedge, mile-a-minute,
  creeping Cinderella—

from the cracked soil, and it will be
  impossible not to think

of people lost when soft galaxies of earth
        are revealed beneath
        what she sees,

the ones who should have enjoyed more
        almost-mild March afternoons

The succulents have exploded across
        summer along with all the other things

that need no tending, no care, that create
        an unnatural healthy blur
        against the scorched lawn

Beyond this place are stars and planets,
        comets kicking footballs across astral fields

She likes to think of them—a rumble
        of distant applause

that will always sound like storm clouds splitting,
        rain splashing to earth

Lonely Poem

In arcane sunlight I sit in a gazebo
on the northern city fringe
contemplating first lines.
Poems are lonely
but necessary at times like this:
they keep me in check
so the day's colours might
seep into an inventory of hope.

*

I write poems to know where the hills are,
how the leaves turn before a December storm,
whether light is slanting silver
against that corrugated iron shed
or to describe the desolation
of a sky empty of birds.

*

Once, I thought poetry and love
were the same but now I'm less sure.
I thought a poem was a way of bouncing
exquisite minutiae from mind to mind
across time zones and calendars,
exploring vistas
for mutual understanding,
the way Emily Brontë might have done
from her cold rock on the moors.

*

It is 39 degrees.
I wear dark glasses,

drink iced water from a flask,
contemplate endings.
My son phones to tell me he is locked out of the house,
that the dog is barking hysterically,
that he is hot,
has lost his key.

*

There are subplots in this poem.
Whole chapters.
The morning's edges are curling.
No one knows
that I am here in this park
except a crow circling in a wide sweep of heat
and the poem I have just given life to.

Lunch on Stormy Day with Visible and Invisible Lines

In the food court palms carry overweight clouds in concave arms—
the sky is leaden and stamped with crow song.
_____

Students queue at a burger bar as a legion of the dark birds
hop, watching for abandoned tables.
_____

She eats a saffron spiced cauliflower salad that matches
the yellow hospital windows and the colour of the tram paused at the
crossing.
_____

She is remembering a post she saw earlier where a queue of people
line up across a field waiting to turn from solid to platinum to invisible
_____

as they arrive at the point of uplift, rising above trees and buildings,
becoming lost in atmosphere
_____

Two people she knows have died in the last twelve hours—
neither knew they were at the front of that queue
_____

yet the bird near her feet with the peridot eyes is disturbingly alive
waiting for any drop or spill
_____

and the jasmine sprawling in long beds between cafes is seething with life
and students are pointing at the neon sign advertising $16 cocktail share
jugs—
_____

glistening yellow drinks in haloes of purple surrounded by hearts—
and they are laughing while nurses and doctors rush back from lunch to
preserve life
_____

There are lines of people everywhere—for Mexican food, for coffee, for trams and buses, cars snaking around the corner as they wait to enter the hospital carpark

———————

and now the sun is breaking through and she is walking to the classroom and she has surrendered her table to the crows

————————————————————————

From the West Wing

The hospital sits within a concentric circle of time: through
the window a black bird

sits in a white-trunked tree, a vacant car park sprawls, a train
hurtles by, a sunless day

sucked of joy is suspended grey on a hanger. I have special
powers: can see forward and back,

remember the future in fine cartographic lines—jigsaws of
boats that blur to become animals

drawn with fingers on hot sand. There are coastlines of touch,
a vulnerability in the face

of sharp pointed instruments — I am reminded of miracles:
the small happy cloud I lived on mothering

two small boys. You endlessly scroll on your phone and I turn
the pages of a book with images

of temporal sculptures from water, ice, leaves, feathers. It occurs
to me that we live in a world

that is both hard and soft: not easy to distinguish between them.
The magenta wall of this room

is an unkind industrial colour. You sleep, half-turned away and
your lashes sweep a cheek moments ago

an angry red. Time is a stretch of nerve fibres: anticipation and regret.
Across the river, first lights blink.

Incantation

I don't know the name of the beach
where I'm standing: there's a giddiness
of the world being new again,
anything possible, and a tiny theft
of pleasure like anticipation when
I know the sun will reemerge
from behind clouds strewn above
the bolt of zaffre water, across amber-
leaf mangrove rooftops.
                        An incantation
of salt tongues and I wonder if this
mud-stained circle is where crabs
meet? The tide is at crossover
and there's a feeling of time running
out—it happens a lot lately even
when the sea isn't ebbing—
in the distance, the Glasshouse
Mountains are turning from phthalo
to mauve.
               I imagine tonight's stars
of iron pyrite reflected in this polished
passage of ocean, the thin beach curve
of sand and shingle drowned black.
Emotions are messages to the muscles
and I walk, notice calligraphic people
sitting under lazy eucalypts—
some tightly scribbled, hard-pressed,
others formed of bouncing tendrils
that escape their outlines.
                           At a bend
in the path, a man stands at an easel
painting a landscape in time-bomb
strokes and I know I must return
to the car, to the bridge, to the mainland.

Pure colours are separated by zones
of uncertainty and I wonder if this day
is the middle of eternity, at its end
or just at the very start? Reading
my thoughts, two pelicans glide
beneath the stippled cotton trees,
perch on the pale shore.

Fugue

There's a dotted line
between where she ends and the rest
of the world begins,
where those otherworldly creatures
she loves live like pets.
      She feeds them.
      She drives them where they need to go.
      She gives them advice in a voice
that sounds like her own.

There's a slow damage of words
not falling:
the air is heavy with their absence.
The realm of imagination
has betrayed her.
By luck, she lives in a house surrounded
with enchanted trees
where aureolin birds nest.
She envies their levity and light
      across the divide
      as they take off into the cosmos,
into a cool, wide expanse of what looks blue.

From the Attic

I thought a lot about the maze of rooftops—
    the slopes and gussets and gutters.
        Not everyone knew the place that way.

The groan of lilac was loudest in spring—
    a beauty of excess—corrugated iron
        scattered with petals, roof corners piled

purple deep, the dedication of honey-
    eaters I watched skim silver to their nests.
        Around dusk, the floodlights at Albion Park

flickered to life, reflections pooled
    on the low flat roof beside the trellis,
        the scent of jasmine wafting up,

and I tried not to dwell on the warmth
    of home—where you were—of lights
        in places I couldn't see, listened instead

as the river breathed along to dark
    beats, to the silence of stained glass
        after sun. I'd prop against the timber

casing when a leaden sky edged menacing
    green, wait for the battering of rain
        on glass, for water to glug through roof

canals so I'd sleep—imagine other rivers,
    other storms. So being there was
        softened by a kind of abstraction.

Spinning Coin, 1993

Kneeling on sandpaper carpet squares
we unpack boxes of Helmut Newton & Herb Ritts.
Body & Soul is playing

& she is telling me about *The Volcano Lover*—
an inventory of desire— but I am hardly listening.
You should read it, she says,

but I receive a dozen good recommendations a day.
The Friday night gang are browsing, or paying
for long-wanted brown paper packages.

The bookshop is a forest at night
but one where I know all the fairytale endings.
This city is too steamy and safe.

Soon, I am flying away.

I have a torn magazine picture of a wild Cornwall coast
on the fridge of my share house,
have read *Rebecca* 18 times.

When I finally leave, he will stand in the street & wave
until he can no longer see a speck of me.
I will turn at least ten times—wave back

but also be the first not to /
I don't buy a book for months & months
until I find *The Shipping News* & read
that *a spinning coin, still balanced on its rim,*

may fall in either direction.

Through a Car Window

A woman walks through the luscious park.
I suppose she might be unpacking
the history of sunshine and love
because there are excerpts around her—
gold filigree blossoms pinned to the trees,
a molten path
                or might her head be
worry-crammed and aching? Her face
is turned away and her strides
across the lawn might well be to free herself
from tragedy or weigh up two sides
of a debate
                or she might be only half-
noticing the hidden crows in the foliage
or the cumulous cloud far off, foreshadowing
a storm late in the day
                        most likely,
this brightly dressed woman is asking herself
if she will ever amount to anything more
than a beeswax body, her experiences
conditioned by the filter of her words,
hours later, at the desk in the dark room
where her colour is hidden,
where the light can't reach
her philophobic heart.

The World is Cruel and Lovely

Driving across town I hear the jacarandas in Crosby Road
    before I see them: an opera of lilac.
The road vibrates and the sun is butter.
    Blake said that that the tree which moves some
to tears of joy is, to others, only a thing
    that stands in the way…
a neighbour will cut down a violet tree because the blossoms
    make a mess on the path.
Beauty is a headache repeating constantly, and especially now
    when what's near seems larger.
The world is both cruel and lovely. In photographs,
    I want to capture the exact way
a grove of trees looks in a particular month, or season,
    or time of day.
The pictures crowd my phone. The humming sound of the colours.
    Time fragments that pass
in a different way to before. The green feathers of the lorikeet
    on the power pole are the same shade
as the suede of my shoes, and equally, the colour my grandmother
    was most afraid of
so she is captured, somehow, in the scene. Can you see the way
    everything is connected?
She wore navy, always, and a cerise cardigan of cashmere,
    the swirling brown river the colour of her eyes.

Grounded

There's no brown snake
   about the blue river today.
     It holds its own against
       ignimbrite cliffs, mossy parks,
    the ivory murmuring of boats.
  Wrapped in its corners
for years, I try and envision
a life we might have had
  in Antigua or Rhodes
    but that is like imagining
      this wide meander without
      mangroves and bull sharks,
    its synclines and anticlines,
  tributaries and hills—
the city's skin and veins
a braille of water and stones.
  Boys wagging school fish
    from the pontoon off Newstead
      Park and an occasional ferry
     cuts the river corner,
    its wash breaking
  on the eyelid of beach
near where I sit, everything
else silent—gulls assembled
  on the grassy rise, electric bikes
    on the walkway, a stout Pekingese
      on a lead, a couple of picnickers
    sleeping off lunch, palm trunk
  shadows striping my feet.

Vernissage

The trees are witches' brooms. Their reflections
sweep the still surface.

She closes her eyes on sunset as cockatoos squall
in the boughs above her,

talks sternly to herself. These mercurial moods
must stop. After all,

the day's edge is purled in gold. It was one of those
annoying social media

memes that delivered the cledon, as if on a pillow
of silk, then a friend's

life cut short. The time of expectation had to pass.
Clusters of ancient stars

begin to emerge on the far shore fringed by palms
the shape of hand

prints pressed against the vast sky: a canvas
of chance.

Night on Prison Island
for Alastair
after our visit to St Helena Island in Moreton Bay, 2018

Wallabies dream in a honeyed night
garden of crocus and sweet alyssum.
Do they see the sad souls of those
who never left this prison paradise?

Beneath a warder moon, gold
and watchful above the roofless
beach-rock walls, the ghosts rise
in white, traipse in single, silent file

through neglected olive groves
at the rhythmic bidding of the tides.
Cows low to the mournful stories
of stars, needles rasp as rough hands

push thread to sew sails, the white
figures huddled cross-legged now
under Moreton Bay fig trees until
just before dawn. Little girls in white

lace frocks play solemn hopscotch
on the beach near the headstones,
supervised by waxbills and curlews.
In their visions, the wallabies coax

them to ride on their backs, keep
ghost babies warm in their pouches
on icy winter nights, but their young
eyes don't smile. They were left behind

on this island to the eternal gossip
of dugongs and bats, noisy school-
children by day, the smell of shell
burning to make lime, sugar boiling,

parents' broken goodbyes. Their only
crime—that they were St Helena
children. The wallabies wake, at last,
to the honesty of the sun, the grass sweet
and cool in the long shadows of the ruins.

Unbreakable Line

An oak tree divided twelve times:
window frames like knives
at first light

Can the parts of us that remain
survive rememberings
of the past?

Wheel flowers decay under ice
but thought furies spin:
topiary displays

and miniature boxed hedges can't
sustain new myths
Clouds appear

at my feet, pacing the banks
of another muddy river,
light rain

washing red marks away from a décor
of wrinkled wood, branches,
natural stone,

new inventories of distance holding
us apart, twitchy conversation
following meanders

and falls, bush paths intersecting,
twisted stories of people
I thought I knew well

At some point, I can only think
of death, its unbreakable
line becoming

every ripple in the water,
the bruised sky breaking,
and later

each pane of glass a maligned face
backlit by lightning
against the oak

Survey

A young man with a clipboard asks me, as I stand poolside about to immerse myself in invisibility, about how I might feel if another swimmer was unhappy to share a lane and requested that I move, and whether if this situation was to present itself, I would refuse or immediately agree? If I consider I have equal rights to someone who might be a stronger swimmer? Or would think their need was greater? And if I agreed, would it be to avoid confrontation, or because it was my duty to move (I had already admitted that I didn't think myself a strong swimmer) or because I am a complete pushover no matter what demands are made of me?

All of this before I have even dipped my toe in the water on a Monday morning. And if you don't mind me asking (this is for an official university study, he continues) why is it that you come here to swim? Is it for training or fitness or health or relaxation or to take a break from your routine or as a change from another kind of exercise or for your mental health? Just for fun maybe?

I don't tell him that I love the raised pavilion and the curvilinear walls, the startling composition of geometric and plastic modernist-influenced forms that let me feel as if I am moving through an alien landscape in fluid, transparent space at a futuristic junction, that the teal and white bunting creates a festive air that buoys me while at the same time supporting, restoring, that if I close my eyes I can almost imagine I'm in a clear, azure Mediterranean swathe of smooth sea surrounded by craggy cliffs and molten-warmed, that there is nothing more optimistic than to make fresh strokes through a newborn, mist-covered pool as the sun appears, so a new day is an invention all of my own and skin becomes water that becomes a rhythm of me and my mind moving yoga-like, worry draining so an amniotic feeling returns me to untroubled times far from the struggle on land, and that toxins are released despite the water not being salt and because Hippocrates' beliefs about water and healing are somehow unquestionably true.

I don't tell him, either, that the silence of swimming is not nothing, that silence is not empty or meaningless, that the black line I follow is not part of any grid, that noise cannot control me where I go, that aqua is a friend that unspools my clogged head so sentences appear already formed on a deep page, that every exhalation helps me shed poison, that I swim to find a softer understanding, that I saw a video of a deer swimming between Scottish islands at low tide and that sometimes I imagine myself to be that deer, with its fragile litheness and that despite not looking particularly lithe, I use the time to ponder questions about whether humans really did evolve from fish – quite hard to imagine as we only negotiate the rough interface between atmosphere and fluid with feet that act a bit like brakes, and that sometimes you don't need a reason.

I am conscious this answer is too long to fit on the earnest young man's clipboard.

4

What Starts & Ends with Space

Watching hang gliders with Leonardo da Vinci at Tamborine Mountain

We look for solutions in the sky—
a relentless quest—

From here on the still-
warm western escarpment grass
the valley is a salad
of farms and small settlements
under Renaissance clouds

Thresholds are closer here:
figuration/abstraction: cloud cover/rain
and there are wounds in the air—
a lack of answers from beyond
an invisible wall

As the next glider
waits for the windsock
I study Leonardo's face—
weather-worn but with bird-keen eyes
that see angles and angels,
that are portals to batwing dreams
and electric-blue-thermal days

He is difficult to read
but we talk about progress, the way
his wing-seeds took life and sprouted
despite the earth-locked severity of his time,
ideas that dipped and rose
over centuries

He tells me things—
the function of feathers and their intricate designs,
the action of a falcon's tail,
the way a sparrow moves, steers, dives,

ascends in flight
and the way an eagle's vision
multiplies colour by five

Sometimes I see in ultraviolet too, I tell him,
an infrared riot of colours,
make sense of things using wave-
lengths, and I ask him if thinking
is a kind of flying,
like riding a bike through air
free of sepia burdens before they're mirror-written
in a lasting codex?

Whether painting is a way of dreaming when awake?

I offer him figs and wine
while he recounts a story
about the Duke of Milan's payment
of a vineyard for *The Last Supper* back in 1498—
but this makes him sad because the place is a museum now
and the wine, he says, has lost its softness—

the world has lost its softness—

I may not see him again

It is his turn to soar from the luscious green ridge
and he is sliding gloves over those expressive
ink-stained hands,
reading my mind

He reminds me not to forget the relationship between
the forces that pull down
and lifting pressure on a bird's wing,
that the air is fluid and so am I,
that the light is thickening to dusk and autumn is visible
because trees are reddening

and there is a deep fuchsia-clarity towards the horizon
which is an empty line demanding words

Sketch: Creek Lane Maryborough, 1978

You: cycling
along the laneway
beside the garden
where hundreds of mignonette lettuce grow—
two in your basket—
change jangling in your pinafore pocket
cassia trees in flower
bougainvillea climbing trellises
three stray cats watching
from a tank stand
behind the butcher shop
the yellow green of the verge
is beautiful to you:
the dust you're raising
part of a magic of belonging
it is summer and your feet are bare
your hat has fallen on the stony path
behind but you don't know or care
there has never been anything else
but sun really
and the effortless moving
of your legs

Why this Messy Blue Paradise?

There are no flying lovers

in the sky even though it is purple
and the branches hang upside down

but vague shapes in garden corners
might be Chagallian beasts

wreathed in boronia
and bottlebrush

burnt sienna pinks
in the gum's noisy bark

    Today I can't remember
    the shape of your lips

    but don't you think
    the wildness of love
    is the most orphic thing?

Soon rain will fall
in the ninth storm in nine days

globs of red brick blurring
against mosaic strokes

of umber and cream
where courtyard meets walls:

the motif of looking out a window
unavoidable, tragic—

>   your deepest thoughts
>   still voids to jump—

The garden is a mood piece

but for a moment
as some last brilliance flashes
on glass

I imagine that painting where a man

parachutes through an orange sky
clutching a triangle

each compartment of the scene
divided

>   and though I can't
>   see his face
>   I know he is smiling.

Elysian

I go to the field where the artists are said to be:
thousands of rows of half-worked paintings
on easels stand beside plain wooden beds
like the one Vincent had in Arles. The occupants
stand holding their palettes and brushes
or sleep untroubled. There are tables with bowls
of fruit and flowers, a view of mountains
and a river winding through a valley, far off
forest trees and a sorrowful sky complicated
by last sun that Constable would have studied
closely for emotion. I walk for hours searching
for my father as it slowly darkens, checking each
of the taped works for style and signature.
No-one seems to speak—but it's an amicable
silence. Nor does it rain so the once-artists
sleep beneath the stars. I lose count of how long
I search before I find him. The fox terrier he had
as a child and our family dog are both lying
by his feet while he works furiously by candlelight,
ravaged body lithe, eyes burning. I wonder
if he senses me: impossible to tell, but there is joy
in his face as he mixes yellows, and the sky lightens.

What Starts and Ends with Space

On some days the immensity of sky overwhelms:
empty hillsides that need filling,
meekness of sun or moon or both.

There's a halo above the cane fields so they're alight,
a bandana of cloud scaling the vista
back to a broad wash of marigold and lime.

You hanker for that lost crazy sense of red—probably
how the world looked through younger eyes—
but interrupt the vastness with paint,

wash pigment across textured oatmeal, riff off staccato
words. Black trees make the sky
look bluer. You like the slow combustion,

the sprung rhythm of bushland when every fourth
or fifth footstep breaks a fallen twig.
You think of Miró saying that a bit of thread

can set a world in motion. Each composition is a place—
real or imagined—so you start with what's small:
chlorophyll flowing through the canal

of a leaf, bark-clamped designs on a rose-coloured
trunk, the tangerine hides of cows
moving against navy-shadowed

brigalow trees in a way that makes complete sense.
Sometimes it's good to tilt the landscape,
to imagine the place you're in from the air instead

so the hills have a chance to echo. You pray
for happy accidents like unintentional
backruns in wide, buttery backgrounds.

Light pressure with the tip of a pointed brush will give
you a precision of memory like the steep
arch of the Milky Way hours later

as you sit by the window, recollecting other frames,
feeling the universe throb, taking
the rapid pulse of shooting stars as they fall.

Afterlife
inspired by Jeffrey Smart's 'The Oil Drums', 1992

I think of Exxon Valdez, Deepwater Horizon.
The glossy public face – its formal geometry

Of slick colour and the artist's golden ratio—
Vivid as a kelp garden teeming with life in the

Bight where they want to drill: cyan, cadmium,
The shrill yellow of unblackened coral, texture

Smooth as honeyed trumpet music. A mastaba
Of greed, a historical set piece, a burning afterlife.

Wrapped

after Christo and Jeanne-Claude's 'Wrapped Coast', Little Bay, Sydney, 1969.

There are films
        of a cherished coast
92,900 square metres of cliff and stone
turned sensuous avalanche
billowing as it met the sea

        of a tousle-haired man standing
unfazed beneath a wuthering sky,
a gyre of clouds around him
and his vast sheets of white:
half event, half monument

Later there would be wrapped
archipelagos and palaces
        absurd cloth-covered epics
a love letter in impassioned fence script
running between states
        the heartbreaking beauty of
orange *furoshiki* trees
partitioning mountains

The memory
of this world turned gallery
is a reminder of what
was beneath

        and perhaps it's time
to wrap the coasts again—
trees, rivers, habitats—
in a gesture of faith
and love
tied with bows
of soft biodegradable rope

Palm Reading

All the blue paintings she has ever seen along an avenue of quiet
dusk colours dipping soft beneath the trees
the faint Morse code
of insects calling from cabbage palms
and steel-tipped Bismark palms
and Canary Island date palms
with invisible high tufts lost in haze
each progressively smaller
across the enamel of night that's beginning to fall
with its grit of regret

Flowers in every garden stare back white
or a Wedgwood interpretation of it:
plumbago, magnolia, stephanotis over gateways
between the endless street
and the abstracted lives,
occasional faceless people floating
above their gabled rooftops
with bouquets of lilac and green
calming babies or cradling family pets

She doesn't regard the road closely or even remember
the blister yellow brassiness of the morning
but wonders what these creatures of suburbia
find in her face,
in her walking here,
in the way she's beginning to slip from sight

It is the palms that read her thoughts:
the far ones are outfielders against distant picket fences
that might not even be real
but close ones mop the sky,
push puddles of stars into corners
so what was written—an inventory of what matters
that she can't absorb in time—
vanishes

Truths About the Cosmos
after Joan Miró's 'Dancer', 1925

The sky is shedding its skin,
rust at the edges.
Ultramarine this vivid
won't last.
You're more alone, less lonely:
at night, you turn in time
with the moon.
It's no coincidence that begonias
are flowering in bands
of scarlet, orange, white
outlined black,
none still budding, none dead.
There won't be second chances.
See the bee's deft circles?
There's a lightness
you haven't felt
since you were eleven
and dancing.
Miró noticed tiny forms
trapped in vast empty spaces.
Today you opened the leather box,
remembered the red heart-
shaped earring lost
in long grass as you spun
on a Spanish hillside.
You hold the remaining one
in your hand,
its fragile glass beauty
like a late permission to believe
before blue turns to brown.

La Casa Azul

after photographs of Frida Kahlo in her garden

Born from prickly pear, I am.
My seeds were cobalt – cacti mixed
with yucca, agave, canna-lily,
the bougainvillea crown of deep thorny
pink from which pain sprouted.

Selfies grew from blackbird brows,
rouged skin bled into terracotta,
mustard, leaf-green dappled basalt
walls and slabs of raw volcanic rock
that make up a central courtyard

surrounded by the rooms of me –
my eyes weeping shells. Mosaics
that spell my name in a kitchen
of turgid fruits; the glass ceiling
makes sense of my brokenness.

My bathroom a cell of fashionista
loot: red leather boot with leg, bows,
bells, lace *resplandors*, embroidered
Chinese silks, cool *Tehuana huipils*,
enagua underskirts peeking polka dots.

My gallery of *ex-votos*, the re-runs
of tragedy on trolley–buses that crawl
like tin creepers over textured walls
while those painted corsets of misery
sit propped in folk art corners.

My library of botany: tiny bouquets
pressed in chartreuse leaves. A
domestic oasis of portraits, plants,
people, parrots – spider monkeys
scaling the pyramid or my shoulder,

my deer, my pack of dogs cavorting
among pomegranate boughs
and succulents, my meandering pathways
of paint – the comfort and pain
of home and his betrayal mixed *plein air*.

The white crocheted bed where I
assign the colours – soaring pink
of Aztec joy, green of sadness, yellow
of madness and fear, the cut red
of melon death flesh, that sweet
electricity of my deep blue tender fire.

Tate Cartoon: *I Don't Care! I'd Rather Sink Than Call [X] For Help!*
after Roy Lichtenstein

We stood in the airless gallery with dozens
of others in front of Drowning Girl.
I could feel sweat against the linen of my shirt,
wanted to shift his hand off my hip.
Don't you think this work is kind of crass? he said.
I didn't want to talk about the subject matter—
men causing women misery—
just enjoy the thick lines and bold colours
with detachment. The Ben-Day dots made her skin
look flawless, framed by her whirlpool of hair.
Earlier in the gift shop, I read that Brad
wasn't always absent:
before Lichtenstein cropped the image,
he was in the background holding the catamaran
while she dealt with a cramp in her leg.
I didn't allude to the fact that the artist's
first marriage was dissolving as he painted it.
As we walked silently towards Blackfriars afterwards,
we were the clichéd ones,
thought bubbles stacked above our heads.

Girl with 1,000 Faces
after Piero Fornesetti's 'Face of Lina Cavalieri', 1952

At the train station, he re-makes my world in a familar-strange way. Pieces fall everlastingly slowly: platforms lead nowhere and have fake symmetries. I collect words from unknown works to greet other passengers and each wears his expressionless woman's face. She sits opposite me—no warmth in her smile, just possibility. Are her gloves disembodied hands? Fish caught between her fingers? Her clothes are printed with antiquated typefaces of the nineteenth century. Shell landscapes adorn the carriage walls with group portraits of creatures from the deep. The train eventually pulls to a stop with a great monochromatic shudder of anticipation. In the city, a poetry of ruins and lost grandeur, ancient piazzas and complicated columns, metaphysical shadows across floors of stone. I meet him for coffee in an emporium that seems to dance. We sit in lyre-back chairs, a vase of newsprint roses on the tiger table between us. His pet unicorn kneels in a corner. He wears one of his beautiful scarves that is a Baroque palace, its multi-story design climbing up his body to his mustachioed face. We order coffee, cake that arrives in lobster and octopi shapes. One whole wall is a painted aviary with generously spaced bars so the birds fly in and out as they please. *Don't be alarmed*, he says, unhinging the back of his head to reveal a cupboard full of fantastic games. He shuffles cards, places them before me in rows: lid=roof; plate = maze; flower = mouth; pocket = window. *Nothing has to be as it is. Hold onto the past. Everything will be okay.* I ponder these words later as I step into a bath. His motifs are beginning to fade by this time but the hot and cold taps are still porcelain parrots and there are sideways eyes floating in sud-clouds like fragments of a world invaded by anxiety. Hot air balloons are embossed on the ceiling, blown about by cornices of sun. I float above identities, realities, exquisite details of the day warding off a dread of nothingness, a whole banal world exploding into air.

You do not see less by looking at a field out of focus with a magnifying glass
after Gerhard Richter

The immense book of paintings
on the coffee table
is best navigated
on a sunny day
when dark revelations
are part of the morning's
soothing and streaking

> *blur makes all the parts*
> *a close fit*
>
> *a fuzzy gaze focuses*
> *the mind*

He makes us choose
between a feeling
and a photograph

so these mysteries in grey
or dull green
help me remember
a squeegee through the multilayer
flatbed of my own past—

the curved scope
to where my horse stood
in wintery mist
then cantering to my call
through ferns and tubular branches

the animated outlines
of spider webs tracing
the lunge yard post corners

Composition was a side issue then too—

mornings at the paddock
were more pure chance
than autobiography

more aurora
of neighbouring sunlit airfield
than simple stain
of molasses on chaff

a trope for the illusion of youth
or wholesomeness?

ancient values of meaningfulness?
pleasure?

Seat in the saddle
or the warm bare back
knees inward, holding firm

me versus outside forces

a field with long grass and sunrise
in close photographic detail

or sweep of freedom, lost?

The End of the Experiment

There are places that stifle your thinking,
places where you need to hoard your thoughts
for upcoming disasters—
      switch the lights on,
      insert the right code,
      make sure the doors are armed,
      that the art won't fall from the walls

The artifice of some paintings
crowd out words you might have written
so you can feel reduced to the suggestion
of a person who can't dream past
someone else's worthiness

Now that you've handed back the keys,
have permission to be free,
you take the long way round
on the drive home,
slowing
beside the shallow green water
with its copper reflections
and meanders that catch white stones

To your right
there are still distant smokestacks
and warehouses
but as the road curls closer to town along the ridge
the citrus-faced houses and pink-scalloped lawns
begin to unroll like felt,
all the trees of suburbia
resting against a wimple of purple hills—
it's a kind of release:
you feel neurons connecting
and synapses flowing back

You navigate the tangle of freeways
that are a fluorescent spaghetti
and ideas pop again like corn
when you pass the high-key colours of shops
and cinemas and restaurants
and new cars for sale wrapped in bows

A new poem's title is woven
into the sunset's strange welcome

Acknowledgements and Notes

My thanks to the editors of the following publications where many of these poems first appeared, sometimes in other versions:

Antipodes, Coastlines, Cordite, Hecate, Inkfish, Live Encounters, London Grip, Noon: Journal of the Short Poem, Other Terrain Journal, Poetry Salzburg Review, Shearsman, Social Alternatives, StylusLit, Takahē, The Banyan Review, The Blue Nib, The Ekphrastic Review, The Mackinaw, Verity La La, Westerly, Faith: 2024 ACU Prize for Poetry Anthology (ACU 2024), *The Memory Palace* (The Ekphrastic Review 2024), *Poetry of Change: The Liquid Amber Prize Anthology* (Liquid Amber Press 2024), *Poetry for the Planet: An Anthology of Imagined Futures* (Litoria Press 2021) and *The University of Canberra Health Poetry Prize Anthology* (UC 2024). 'The Fall,' 'Iris,' 'Survey,' 'Afterlife,' and 'La Casa Azul' were first published in *Wide River* (Calanthe Press 2020) and 'Watching Hang Gliders with Leonardo da Vinci' was first published in the anthology *Ten Poems of Tamborine Mountain* (Calanthe Press 2024).

'Cathexis' responds to Rainer Maria Rilke's lines 'Let everything happen to you; beauty and terror; just keep going; no feeling is final' in the poem 'Go to the Limits of your Longing' in the collection *Book of Hours: Love Poems to God* (1905). In the poem 'Iris,' *rhizome* is a philosophical concept developed by Gilles Deleuze and Félix Guattari in their *Capitalism and Schizophrenia* (1972–1980) project. It is what Deleuze calls 'an image of thought,' based on the botanical rhizome and connected with ideas about multiplicities. In 'Hobart Reset,' *Dark Mofo* is an annual arts and culture festival in Hobart, Australia, each June that celebrates the Winter Solstice. In 'Oxyrhynchus,' *Oxyrhynchus* is an ancient Egyptian city significant for its discovery of the Oxyrhynchus Papyri. In 'How to be Happier,' *Maman* (1999) is a bronze, marble and stainless-steel sculpture created by Louise Bourgeois. In 'Spinning Coin, 1993,' the line 'A spinning coin, still balanced on its rim, may fall in either direction' is a quote from Annie Proulx's *The Shipping News* (1993). In 'The World is Cruel and Lovely,' William Blake's quote about trees is taken from his written communications with the Reverend John Trusler in 1799. In 'Night on Prison Island,' St Helena Island in Queensland's Moreton Bay has a turbulent history as the site of the state's first penal settlement from 1867–1932. In 'The Girl with 1,000 Faces,' Piero Fornasetti (1913–1988) was a Milanese artist and designer whose 'Tema Variazioni' series featured, as its central motif, hundreds of renditions of opera singer Lina Cavalieri's face. The poem title, 'You do not see less by looking at a field out of focus with a magnifying glass', is a direct quote from German visual artist Gerhard Richter.

I am fortunate in the people who have worked with me to prepare this book for publication. Grateful thanks to Shearsman publisher and editor, Tony Frazer, for his unwavering advice and professionalism. Hugh McMillan and Damen O'Brien read earlier versions of poems in this manuscript and discussed them with me: their talent and generosity helped shape these poems. I also appreciated the friendship and encouragement of poets Stephanie Green, Nathan Shepherdson, Jena Woodhouse, Rosanna Licari, Victoria Bladen, Lisa Collyer, Esther Ottaway, Brett Dionysius, Melissa Ashley, Margaret Clifford, Matt Hetherington, Vanessa Page and David Terelinck as this book evolved. Thanks to my son Euan Cummiskey for his inspired cover design. Love and thanks, as always, to my family and friends.

www.ingramcontent.com/pod-product-compliance
Lightning Source LLC
Chambersburg PA
CBHW031635160426
43196CB00006B/433